A litt

Su   ey
Memories

Personal memories inspired by The Francis Frith Collection®

THE FRANCIS FRITH COLLECTION

www.francisfrith.com

Based on a book first published in the United Kingdom in 2013 by The Francis Frith Collection®

This edition published exclusively for Bradwell Books in 2013
For trade enquiries see: www.bradwellbooks.com or tel: 0800 834 920
ISBN 978-1-84589-720-8

British Library Cataloguing in Publication Data

A Little Book of Surrey Memories
Personal Memories inspired by The Francis Frith Collection

The Francis Frith Collection
Oakley Business Park,
Wylye Road, Dinton,
Wiltshire SP3 5EU
Tel: +44 (0) 1722 716 376
Email: info@francisfrith.co.uk
www.francisfrith.com

Printed and bound in Malaysia
Contains material sourced from responsibly managed forests

Front Cover: **FARNHAM, THE BOROUGH 1924** 75293t
Frontispiece: **SALFORDS, THE SCHOOL 1907** 57630

The colour-tinting is for illustrative purposes only, and is not intended to be historically accurate

A little book of Memories – A Dedication

This book has been compiled from a selection of the thousands of personal memories added by visitors to the Frith website and could not have happened without these contributions. We are very grateful to everyone who has taken the time to share their memories in this way. This book is dedicated to everyone who has taken the time to participate in the Frith Memories project.

It is comforting to find so many stories full of human warmth which bring back happy memories of "the good old days". We hope that everyone reading this book will find stories that amuse and fascinate whilst at the same time be reminded of why we feel affection for Britain and what makes us all British.

Francis Frith always expressed the wish that his photographs be made available to as wide an audience as possible and so it is particularly pleasing to me that by creating the Frith website we have been able to make this nationally important photographic record of Britain available to a worldwide audience. Now, by providing the Share Your Memories feature on the website we are delighted to provide an opportunity for members of the public to record their own stories and to see them published (both on the website and perhaps in our books), ensuring that they are shared and not lost or forgotten.

We hope that you too will be motivated to visit our website and add your own memories to this growing treasure trove – helping us to make it an even more comprehensive record of the changes that have taken place in Britain in the last 100 years and a resource that will be valued by generations to come.

John M Buck
Managing Director

www.francisfrith.com

A little book of...

The Launderette

I remember this picture very well. Just down the road from
Woolworths by the white car, was a Launderette (maybe
it's still there). This Launderette was the first one ever
introduced to the UK from America in 1959. As we had no
washing machine or dryer, this place certainly changed our
lives. I can remember one day I was with my brother Bernard
waiting for the washing and as usual went to look for some
mischief (this time in Woolie's). On this particular day they
were selling mousetraps for three pence each. Just for some
fun we set each one (without cheese!) and watched with great
amusement as customers picked them up and nearly had their
fingers broken. Naturally we got caught and received a well
deserved clip round the ear by the store manager.

Dudley Piggott

Weybridge, High Street c1955 W74049

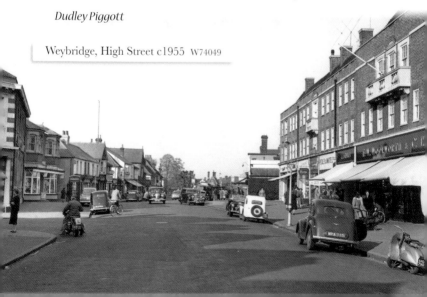

Mac May

Ashtead, The Fish Pond 1904 52587

I lived in a cottage by this pond some 25 odd years ago. My neighbour, well into her 90s, was Mac May (a version of her true name garbled by other neighbours' kids) who, every day, was out in her

> "The little girl is Mac May and her brother has just thrown the milk jug at her."

wellies digging in the garden. We had this photo and, knowing Mac May had lived in the cottage all her life, asked if she knew the children. She did and she remembered the photo being taken. The boy and the girl in the middle are Mac May's elder brother and sister; the little girl is Mac May herself and her brother has just thrown the milk jug at her (the small white object in the middle foreground of this view).   *James Moodie*

A little book of...

The Doodlebug

When I was born in 1939 we lived at 97 Shelvers Way, but my very first memory happened in 1944 during the war. It was a lovely sunny day and my mother, Doris Parker, was going to feed the chickens at the bottom of the garden. I was playing outside when mother called out to tell me to go inside and into the shelter as there was a 'funny' thing in the sky. I never did get to the shelter, only the dining-room, and the next thing I remember was a great bang, glass flying everywhere and a crystal fruit bowl on the sideboard exploding. A doodlebug (flying bomb) had landed in the field opposite our house, causing quite a lot of damage. Soon a WVS (Women's Voluntary Service) van arrived to help, mainly, I think, by dispensing cups of tea, but what I remember most of all is our neighbour, Mrs Everington, giving me a sugar lump, something I'd never even seen before!

Ann Chapple

Tadworth, Shelvers Way c1955 T1016

The Parade in the 1950s

I lived in a flat over 12 The Parade (then a Garden Shop) until I was ten years old, from 1944-1954. Our gate was on the alley round the back. At the Hare Lane end of the alley were hung 'pig bags' - sacks where people put scraps to feed pigs (post-war, so still on rationing!). The other end of the alley went through to one of the brickyards that were then still around Claygate. A rag-and-bone man came along The Parade every week, perched on a horse-drawn shallow cart; we called him the 'Yak-Yoh man' because that was what his 'ragandbone' cry sounded like.

> "We called him the 'Yak-Yoh man' because that was what his 'ragandbone' cry sounded like."

Pat Verral

Claygate, The Parade 1952 C519018

Paper boy – A Memory from the 1950s

As a 12-year-old I sold newspapers every morning outside the cookhouse of the barracks at Caterham where hundreds of National Servicemen were going through the horrors of their initial training in the Guards regiments. I believe they earned 28/6 per week, much of which they had to spend on boot polish, Brasso and Blanco! Their breakfasts looked pretty disgusting - porridge, greasy fried grub and then bromide-laced tea - all in the same mess tin. All the regiments had their own bands, so the sound of marching music echoed around Caterham on the Hill nearly every day. They had their mascots too - I really fancied owning the Irish Guards' wolfhound. Recruits used to go in, in their Teddy Boy drapes - and not emerge for eight weeks, by which time they would have been transformed into disciplined, clockwork men! After this preview of life in the Army, it's no wonder that 3 years later I joined the Royal Navy!

Francis Younghusband

> "Recruits used to go in, in their Teddy Boy drapes - and emerge transformed into disciplined, clockwork men! "

Caterham, The Barracks 1951   C49032

Redhill, Station Road East 1906 55033

A Memory of Redhill swimming baths and town

Does anyone remember the old swimming baths at Redhill? I started swimming there in the 1970s when it was still a Victorian building. The steps in the pool were of stone and the changing rooms were around the poolsides with wooden doors. You could pay to have a slipper bath! There was a young lady who gave you a box to put your clothes in and you had to remember the number on it to get it back after your swim. Sometimes we saw cockroaches scuttling on the floor. I joined the swimming club 'The Marlins' and trained every Thursday with Mrs Ditzel. She seemed rather fierce at the time but she was just trying to get the best out of us. I also remember certain little shops along Station Road, a lovely old-fashioned chemist and a children's clothes shop called Hancock and Bean. There was a nice boutique near there which sold Mary Quant clothes which my mother used to love. I was really sad when Redhill changed so much in the 1980s. It seemed to lose so much character.

> "A young lady gave you a box to put your clothes in and you had to remember the number on it to get it back."

Angela Middleton

Cards, cornettos and the cage

If you hadn't fallen in the pond, you were not from Lingfield! So says my dad. The building to the right of the Cage (the name for the old village prison) in the photo of Lingfield on pages 12-13 was a shop. My memory of this shop only goes back to the mid 1970s. My grandparents' house was behind the shop (the hedge to the right on the photo is the edge of their property), and whilst on holiday visiting them, my brother and I would play cards with Granddad for 5p a hand. He always claimed that he 'was the best pontoon player in the world' although he would always twist on 18+! We always managed to win and when we both got up to 50p we would always run down the garden path and go to the shop and buy a Cornetto. My dad was born in the house and we would go back every 2 or 3 years but now my grandparents are both gone and this photo is a great memory. During the late 1970s in the punk era a load of punks used to congregate around the Cage. One time my nan had had enough of the noise of them and their bikes, so she threw a bucket of water over one of them. They rode off and my nan made the front page of the East Grinstead Courier. She sent the paper over to us and I ran across the road and showed my auntie from my mother's side. I got a chocolate because we were a brave family. (I wasn't more than 8 years old.)

Rod Swift

The Village I Knew

I used to live at Raymead in Lingfield which was a complex of 24 prefabs, they have been replaced now by a new estate. I come back to Lingfield every year to see the village I grew up in. We used to walk to the village pond at night and there was one night at Christmas when it was snowing and they had put fairy lights round the tree by the prison, it looked so lovely I will always remember it as long as I live. I lived there from 1942 - 1965.

Lydia Peyton

"If you hadn't fallen in the pond, you were not from Lingfield!"

Lingfield, The Old Prison and the Pond c1955 L50009

The Old Cottage

The cottage seen in the photograph on pages 16-17 was in Bedford Lane in Frimley Green. I lived in a house called Connemara, which still stands in Bedford Lane. My father, Samuel Richardson, and his brother George were bricklayers. They had the job of demolishing this cottage and they were burning the thatch. My brother John was playing dare. He walked through the outer edge of the white ash of the fire and dared me to walk through the middle. Unfortunately I did, and was very badly burned. Mother rushed round all the houses, collecting tealeaves to put on my legs. (In those days people didn't empty their pots after every brew – they just topped them up with a little more tea and hot water.) I still do not know where Mother got the idea of the tealeaves, but it certainly worked. I was left with just a few little scars, and they are hard to find. After demolishing the cottage, Father and Uncle George built a pair of red brick houses. A Mr Fairminer lived in the first of the pair, and I went to school in Frimley Green with his son.

Mr D F Richardson

> "He walked through the outer edge of the white ash of the fire and dared me to walk through the middle."

Blast From The Past

Wow, did that ever shake me to the core when I read Mr Richardson's memory about Frimley Green on the Frith website. The names Richardson and Fairminer, Long and a few others sprang to mind as fellow pupils at the local Primary School. In those days I lived in Worsley Road. I can remember fishing the Basingstoke canal at Frimley Green and seeing the last barge go by which I believe was scuttled just before the flight of locks.

John Oxford

My Grandparents' Home

I received information from my cousin Leslie about the photo on the following pages on the Frith website. Now that I have seen it I am delighted. My grandparents were Thomas Benjamin Fairminer (1881-1954) who married Louisa Florence Smith (1880 - 1944). They raised 11 children, some of them at Bedford Lane. Their birth dates range from 1900 to 1924. My mother Florence Louisa (known as Ciss) was born in 1905. I remember visiting Bedford Lane as a very young child, one of my mother's brothers, Alfred, lived a couple of houses down. A Mr D F Richardson shared information about this photo on the Frith website in April 2006. He says that he went to school with one of Mr Fairminer's sons, who must have been one of my uncles. I wonder which one it was? I am researching my mother's family and I have been able to get in touch with a number of cousins, many of them and their families still live in Frimley Green and in areas close by.

Joyce Hunt, Queensland, Australia

Frimley Green, An Old Cottage 1906 54907

The Golden Farmer

I used to live in Maultway North - the turning directly to the right of the Jolly Farmer - in the mid 1980s, so I have hazy memories of the pub as a customer. But I remember feeling the place to be cut off from the rest of the world - it was always a challenge crossing the London Road as the pub is now smack bang in the middle of a busy roundabout, a million miles away from this tranquil image. The legend of the Golden Farmer (where the pub gets its name) always fascinated me - he was a farmer by day but a highwayman by night who robbed rich travellers on their way to London. Famed for paying all his debts in gold, he was eventually caught and hung from the gibbet which stands near the pub, where he was left

> "a farmer by day but a highwayman by night who robbed rich travellers on their way to London."

for all to see. His gold was never recovered and is rumoured to be buried nearby. My efforts towards finding the treasure remain unrewarded! No longer a pub, The Jolly Farmer was first transformed into 'The Mongolian Barbeque', a restaurant. It is now a golf shop.

Julian Hight

Camberley, The Jolly Farmer 1906 57182

A little book of...

Dorking, Boxhill, The Wimpy Bar c1965   D45205

My Weekend Job

WOW, I never thought that I would see this picture again, which used to be a postcard. Yes, that's me doing my weekend job as a waitress at the funky new Wimpy bar on Boxhill. My name was Vanessa Howard and I lived at Ismanola, Boxhill Road. This was reputed to be one of the first Wimpey Bars in the UK, and locals, mods and rockers, and day trippers flocked to buy their Wimpy and Chips and Coffee, Knickerbocker Glory, Pepsi Cola in a glass bottle and all else Wimpy by the thousands. Hot doughnuts were a speciality with queues of folk waiting anxiously for their fix at 4d each or 4 for 1/-. Folk marvelled at the huge picture window which overlooked Dorking. Astute locals would return the glass Pepsi bottles to get the 3d deposit - it was quite a lucrative way of earning a bit of pocket money. Oh - and the washing up on a Bank Holiday was never ending! Situated opposite Upper Farm, the Wimpy bar was previously a tea garden and now is a restaurant.

> 'Locals, mods and rockers, and day trippers flocked to buy their Wimpy and Chips'

Vanessa Burgess

A little book of...

Clipping the hedge at St Anne's
– A memory from the 1950s

My dad, Eric Berry, used to clip this hedge - BY HAND! When we're little, things always seem bigger than they really are, but my recollections of watching my dad clip this hedge on the days he did the gardening at St Anne's Church were pretty accurate. It really is as big as I remember! I also recall going to St Anne's Hall (a bit further back down the hill?) with my mum, to collect our ration books. At the bottom of the hill was Fortuna's Ice Cream Parlour - I can still remember the luscious creamy taste! Yum!

Liz Schultz (née Berry)

"My dad, Eric Berry, used to clip this hedge – BY HAND! "

Bagshot, The Church 1906   57176

Saturdays in the cinema

During the Second World War, as youngsters we would look forward to the Saturday morning matinée at the Odeon cinema (4th building on the left of photo). Entrance was thruppence (three pennies). With our pocket money we would splash out on a penny peashooter with a packet of peas. The matinee used to start with a sing-along followed by a cartoon, then two half-hour films, the last being a western serial.

Bad guys always wore the black hats, this was the time for the booing, the good guys wore white hats, this was the time for the cheering. The noise was so loud the cinema manager would come up on the stage to ask the kids to keep the noise down, I'm sure it could be heard half way down the High Street.

John Forder

Epsom, High Street c1955   E37053

23

A Nightingale Sang…

I well remember Banstead station in the 1950s. I used it to
go to school in Wallington from 1953 to 1959 and then to
go to College and then to work in London. At this time I
lived in Nork and of course in those days the trains were
all steam trains. My father used to go to work by train in
the 1940s and always said that at 8.00am, standing on the
platform waiting for the London Bridge train, you could
hear a nightingale sing. Sadly as the station became busier,
this ceased, but it was always one of his abiding memories
of Banstead Station.

Helen Perry

Banstead, The Station c1965 B391114

Royalty at Milford

In 1962 I was in Cledwyn Evans's class at the primary school. In the summer terms Queen Elizabeth the Queen Mother used to visit King Edward's School in Witley, and Mr Evans led his class to the roundabout to see her go by. He was enthusiastically ragged about it by the other teachers! I remember on one occasion we all stood just by the walnut tree on the left of the picture. We waited, but not for long. The Rolls-Royce came whispering up to the roundabout and sailed past us. Then I saw the Queen Mum lean forward to tell her driver to pull up, and he reversed the car back to us. Mr Evans gulped, she waved and smiled at us through the window, then suddenly they were off towards Witley. I noticed Mr Evans was very red faced with excitement!

Mike Taylor

Milford, The Roundabout 1935 86776A

A little book of...

Early morning call

During the Second World War the pupils from this school were evacuated and the building was turned into a temporary Maternity Home. The Doctor attending the home was only part-time, but always on call. The Doctor lived a few houses away and at night time he hung a length of string from a bell next to his bed and out of his bedroom window, so a nurse could run to his house to raise him if he was needed. Such was the case at 2:30am on the 10th of June 1942. I was born shortly thereafter.

John E. Hutt, now living in Lewiston, NY, USA

Ripley, Ripley Court School c1965 R36079

Selmes Butchers

I remember being sent to Selmes the Butchers to buy my mother, Mrs Dora Maynard, cuts of meat. The floor was covered in sawdust and there was a little cashiers' office at the end of the counter. It always had a very friendly atmosphere although I used to cry when I saw the animals being unloaded from the lorries into the slaughteryard. Once or twice I saw them escape.

Helen Swabey (Formerly Maynard)

Bletchingley, The Village Butchers Shop c1935 B122005

Saturday Job

My first job as a Saturday girl (1974) was working at a newsagents called Jarman's on the right of this photo on the corner of the road which led to the police station and infants school, Darley Dene. I remember having to weigh snuff and having to use an old-fashioned till where you had to add up the items and press down the correct keys to show the total in the top window. I worked for a lady called Molly - she was still there in the 1980s. I think I earned about 60p for a Saturday afternoon.

Karen Rogers

Addlestone c1950 A23023

A little book of…

Buy my Lily of the Valley

On one day of the year, through the 1940s and probably the 1950s, my grandmother Ethel Glazier would pick all the lily of the valley she had, in a square bed about three foot square, in her back garden in Rowledge. She would bind them into small bunches, with leaves around, and tie them carefully with thread. They would sit in a bowl of water on the flagged floor of her larder overnight. She would be on the first bus from the village in the morning, and sit in the Castle Street end of this Colonnade, selling the bunches from a basket. She would be home in time for the midday meal, with a pocket full of cash, and a treat of fish heads for the cat (patriotically called Monty). My grandmother was a most respectable woman, and this was totally out of character, but I think she just liked to disprove my grandfather's maxim 'You can't eat flowers!'.

Raela Croft

Farnham, The Colonnade 1936 87793

My Grandma & Aunt

Some years ago I gave my mother a book of Old Weybridge photos for Mothering Sunday as this is where she was brought up. Imagine her surprise, on seeing this picture of Queen's Road in Weybridge, to realise that the two people on the far right were her mother and younger sister, Edith and Lesley Johnson. She recognised her mother instantly from the distinctive hat, which she is also wearing in my mother's wedding photos!

Gill Hicks

"She recognised her mother instantly from the distinctive hat, which she is also wearing in my mother's wedding photos!"

Weybridge, Queen's Road c1955 W74025

Family Day Out - Clerkenwell to Caterham 1925

The photo opposite depicts Dorothy Connor (née Step) aged 10, with her late mother Elizabeth Step (aged 46) and her sister, Florence Step (aged 21) having alighted from the 159a bus which brought them from their home in Clerkenwell, London, pictured outside the Old Surrey Hounds Public House, Croydon Road, Caterham, Surrey on a day out to Caterham in 1925.

They were on their way to the Barracks Hospital to see Dorothy's Uncle Charlie (her father's brother) who was in the army hospital. Wearing a pull-down bonnet and a typical twenties dropped-waist shift, the young Dorothy and her family had no idea they had been caught on camera. It was not until Dorothy was looking through a copy of Helen Livingstone's book about Surrey from The Francis Frith Collection some eighty years on that the exciting discovery was made. Dorothy said: 'My son, Dave, knows I like old books and pictures and as an early birthday present he bought me the 'Surrey Photographic Memories' book. I looked through

> "They were on their way to the Barracks Hospital to see Dorothy's Uncle Charlie (her father's brother) who was in the army hospital."

it and was absolutely flabbergasted; I really couldn't believe my eyes. I showed the photo to my three nieces (Florence's children), who are now in their late seventies, and they were absolutely delighted. We have our own photos of Mum and Florence wearing the same outfits as they were in the Frith photo - it is amazing!' On Dorothy's 90th birthday, there was an article about her in all the local Surrey papers which showed a photograph of her alongside the Frith 1925 photo. The East Surrey Museum also has a copy of the photo in their archives as does the Surrey History Centre at Woking.

Elisabeth Connor

Caterham, Bus in Croydon Road 1925 78135v

A little book of...

Living in the Square at Shere

I was born in July 1940 as Virginia Le Roux. The house on the left of the picture was where I lived until I was nearly 13 with my parents. The long narrow upstairs window was my bedroom. My mother's mother and brother also lived in the house. My uncle – John Grover – had a shop to the left of the porch, where he sold fresh fish, fruit and vegetables, some of which he grew himself. During the Second World War people would come from Dorking and Guildford to buy fresh fish. The fish came from Harlow's of Grimsby in wooden boxes; when the empty boxes were returned to Grimsby, my uncle used to fill them with rabbits and other game caught locally, because food was scarce due to food rationing. My uncle used to smoke kippers in a shed near the stream. He also kept the white ducks which swam along the stream. I have very happy memories of my childhood spent in Shere.

Virginia Pawlyn

> "My uncle – John Grover – had a shop to the left of the porch, where he sold fresh fish, fruit and vegetables, some of which he grew himself."

Shere, The Village 1903 50268

A little book of...

Harvey's Roof Garden

We moved to live in Hersham, Surrey, in the late
1950s and visited Guildford quite often through the
1960s. A visit to the Rooftop Café at Harvey's was
always a highlight for me. I remember jumping from
stepping stone to stepping stone, and watching the
fish darting about in the water. I have never seen
another rooftop café anywhere and I'm very glad to
know this unique place is still in existence – I have
very happy memories of it.

Linda Briggs

Splash

I also have happy memories of Harvey's roof garden
café at Guildford, it was wonderful with frothy
coffee in little glass cups, and we would sit on one
of the 'islands' that the stepping stones in the
photograph led to. I also remember my sister Sue
being about 3 or 4 and falling in the pond head-first
trying to touch the fish, Mum had to dry her out in
the loo.

Bob Whitehead

Guildford, The Roof Garden c1960 G65128

My great-grandfather Harvey Madgwick

My great-grandfather, Harvey Madgwick, was a broom squire in the 1920s, and he lived in a cottage down in the 'bowl' (the Devil's Punch Bowl), as my mother related to me. It was a hard life for these people, but my mother (being brought up by her grandparents) told us many times of the broom squires and their children who lived there.
Frances Hearn

'Broom squires' was the name given to people living in heathland areas who gathered heather, birch and brushwood to make besom brooms, an outdoor brush made from a bundle of twigs tied to a pole (like the 'flying broomstick' traditionally associated with witches). A number of people inhabiting the heathland around Hindhead used to make their living in this way. Besom brooms are still popular with gardeners, and are particularly good for sweeping away fallen leaves.

Hindhead, Broom Squire's Cottage 1907 57877

Jonny 7

Back in the 1960s my sister used to take her dolls to the dolls' hospital in Swan Lane to get them fixed, they also mended teddy bears. My best memory of the dolls' hospital was that they used to have a 'Jonny 7' machine gun set up in the window, it was a toy gun that broke down into 7 different weapons. I was living on Bellfields then and my mum didn't have much money so she couldn't afford to buy me one. All of my mates were in the same boat, so we used to walk to town and spend ages looking through the shop window at it, as often as we could.

Allen Nicol

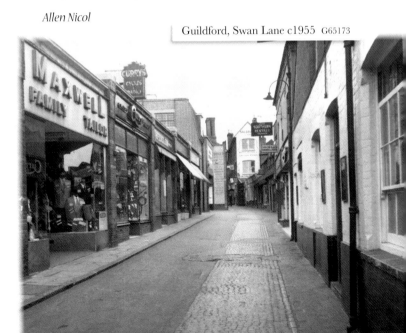

Guildford, Swan Lane c1955   G65173

A little book of...

Kittens under the counter

As a child in the 1960s, I remember the staff in the Co-op store at South Merstham seen in this photograph asking me if I would like to see some kittens, which they produced from a cardboard box kept underneath the counter! The shop is now a hairdressers. The Morris Traveller car (registration XPD600) seen parked by the roadside outside the Co-op in this view belonged to my grandfather, Jack Deverill, who lived in Melton Road.

Anthea Post

South Merstham c1960   S665006

Ryders folklore

These cottages are now known as Ryders, but it appears that in Edwardian times the place (or maybe this corner) may also have been known as 'Seven Trees Well': I have a postcard with this picture on it sent on 7th May 1906 to a Mr Jackson in Victoria Street, London; written on the reverse is 'Do you remember this place (7 tree well)...'. There is indeed a well here – just out of shot to the right. It is said that there is also a connection with the 1963 Great Train Robbery – a picture of some of the robbers standing in the garden once hung in the Punchbowl Inn up the road. (The area does have evidenced Train Robbery connections – £100,000 from the Robbery was found in Coldharbour Woods a few miles away.) The property was once owned by Rex Alston, a legendary BBC commentator in the 1950s and 60s. He co-presented some of the BBC coverage of the Coronation. The property also includes the old village forge, operated by Mr Holden (also of Ockley and Forest Green). Nearby is 'Ruckmans', a grand house designed by Lutyens with a magnificent tree-lined driveway flanked in spring by a spectacular mass of daffodils.   *Gary Crouch*

Oakwood Hill, Sent and Rydersfield Cottages 1906   53525

A little book of…

Wartime Memories of Reigate, Doods Road, 1939-50

In 1940, during the Second World War, my Granny and Grandad Weller, in their cramped semi in Doods Road in Reigate, took me, my mum and dad, my brother and sister plus 2 billeted soldiers under their loving wing, and I can honestly say that was the most happy household you could ever wish for. We knew things were serious when they installed concrete mini pyramids in the street outside which apparently would stop tanks from advancing. I also remember that people flocked to the 'safety' of Reigate Caves to sleep the night and shelter from air-raids, that was crazy on reflection because these are natural sand caves and I suspect one good wallop from a doodlebug that didn't get over the North Downs chalk cliffs would have caved the lot in, thank God it never happened. My father was an entertainer, a good one, highly professional in magic and ventriloquism (he won the UK International Brotherhood of Ventriloquism Cup in the 1950s). He trained me up at the age of 7 to carry out a 15 minute performance on any stage, doing magic using sleight of hand. I hated it but it meant that I did stand in front of 500 people in 1943 in Reigate Caves in full tail suit and patent leather shoes, entertaining people whilst Dorniers and Heinkels droned overhead.

Norman Gardner

Reigate, Castle Caves, The Barons Hall 1886 18972

A little book of…

Memories of the Basingstoke Canal at Frimley Green

I have many memories of the Basingstoke Canal at Frimley Green. I used to swim next to the Kingsmead Bridge. One day I was on the parapet of the bridge, I was grabbing a branch and swinging off the bridge. The branch broke and I hit the bridge wall below. I don't remember any more until I came round. Apparently I was knocked out. I came round and was pushed along by a soldier on a bike, wet through and fuzzy-headed – he saved my life. He told my mother everything, then he didn't give his name and left. I wish I had met him again, he certainly did me a favour. He could have been stationed at Deepcut, Pirbright, Blackdown or Mychett. I'm here today because of him. It was about the late 1940s.

> "The branch broke and I hit the bridge wall below. I don't remember any more until I came round."

I also remember the horse-drawn barges on the Basingstoke Canal at the Kings Head boat house and lock. The barges probably started from Aldershot, and went on through Surrey. I used to wait for the horse and walk under the bridge to the boat house. The bargeman would unhitch the horse

and I would walk with them both to the King's Head pub,
through a gate, turn left and up over the bridge to the lodge
on the other side. I would hold the horse beside the lock. The
bargeman would cross the lock, untie the rope and bring it
back over. I felt really proud holding the bridle of the big horse.
I never felt scared. The bargeman would hitch up and tow the
barge through the lock, over the aquaduct and go on his way.
The barges were huge, all wood, with just enough room to go
through the locks – made to measure.

Mr D R Richardson

Frimley, The Basingstoke Canal and New Boathouse 1909 61829

My Memories of Addlestone

I remember going to fashion shows with a cup of tea and a biscuit in the Co-op in Addlestone on a Saturday. When I was younger the Co-op ran a sports day and we all got a goody box with cream cakes and a surprise of fruit. We shopped at Parrs at the top of the Duke's Head crossroads (seen on the left of this photograph), I can still remember the smell of the cured bacon. Our order was delivered by a man on a bike. Burges the bakers delivered our bread. We had our shoes repaired at Pigotts in Station Road and I went to both day school and boarding school with Dudly Piggot. We went to school on the bus from the bus garage and stood atop the bridge while the trains ran below and engulfed us in steam from the trains below. Airscrew and Weymonds were the biggest local employers. Traylens fun fair came to Addlestone every year, either the last week in July or the first in August. We got our meat from Chambers butchers and I remember Alma Chambers as Carnival Queen, I went to school with her sister Angela. I was the youngest of four children and my brother Mac played for Addlestone Football Club, my dad was the treasurer and my mum served teas on a match day.

Sue Mackender

"...my brother Mac played for Addlestone Football Club, my dad was the treasurer and my mum served teas on a match day."

Addlestone, High Street 1954 A23021

Thursley and the Sailor's Stone

The murder of the sailor at Hindhead has been a tale handed down from generation to generation. My brother was told about it by our dad, who in turn got it from his dad – indeed, if what my brother was told is correct, one of the three murderers was an ancestor of ours! Their names were: Lonergan, Casey and Marshall (Marshall's name was James). I have a copy of a trial document which I obtained from the National Archives and this prompted me to trace our family tree. As yet I have no definite proof that James Marshall was related to me but there is a strong possibility. Apparently only one of the murderers showed remorse for their crime and I like to think that it was James Marshall. I visited the graveyard at Thursley and found the sailor's stone and also visited Gibbet Hill where the three murderers were hanged. None of them were buried – they were left on the gibbet until all that was left were bones which then turned to dust. Some might say a fitting end but I find it rather gruesome.

"– they were left on the gibbet until all that was left were bones..."

Pauline Baldwin

Thursley, The Churchyard, The Sailor's Gravestone 1902 48388

In Memory of
A generous, but unfortunate Sailor,
Who was barbarously murder'd on Hindhead,
On Sep.ʳ 24.ᵗʰ 1786,
By three Villains,
After he had liberally treated them,
And promised them his farther Assistance
On the Road to Portsmouth.

When pitying Eyes to see my Grave shall come,
And with a generous Tear bedew my Tomb;
Here shall they read my melancholy Fate,
With Murder and Barbarity complete.
In perfect Health, and in the Flow'r of Age
I fell a Victim to three Ruffians' Rage;
On bended Knees I mercy strove t'obtain,
Their Thirst of Blood made all Entreaties vain.
No dear Relation, or still dearer Friend,
Weeps my hard Lot, or miserable End.
Yet o'er my sad Remains, (my Name unknown)
A generous Public have inscribed this Stone

A little book of...

One of my favourite fishing spots

This was one of my favourite fishing spots as a youngster in the 1950s. There used to be a bridge over the river here, but the bridge was blown up by the army around 1958. It was a fantastic sight and we rushed over to the river after the explosion to see all the dead fish.

Paul Foster

Hersham, The River Mole c1960 H398021

Watching the Olympic Torch carried through Redhill – for the 1948 London Olympics

I was born in 1940 in Gillingham, Kent, my dad used to work for Short's, the aircraft builders. We moved to Redhill when I was a baby. One of my earliest memories was seeing the Olympic Torch runner coming down Redstone Hill in 1948, for the last time that the Olympics were held in London. I wonder if anyone can remember his name?

We also used to watch the Veteran Cars go through Redhill on the London to Brighton Car Run every year, as they still do, and on a Sunday evening in the summer we all used to go and watch the traffic jam coming back from the coast – we must have been hard up for entertainment! Mind you we didn't have a TV then!

Bruce Cordy

Redhill, Brighton Road c1955 R17026

A little book of…

Bletchingley, On Fair Day 1907 57493x

The Small Boy on the Donkey...

The small boy on the donkey in this photograph is my father,
Arthur Wallis, who was born in 1904 in Bletchingley. The
man standing to the right is my grandfather, Arthur Wallis
senior, born 1862 in Bletchingley. Arthur Wallis senior was the
licensee of the Red Lion Inn and later the proprietor of the
newsagents in the background. The Wallis family came to
Bletchingley in the early 1700s and for 200 years carried out
bricklaying as their trade.

Robert Wallis

FRANCIS FRITH

PIONEER VICTORIAN PHOTOGRAPHER

Francis Frith, founder of the world-famous photographic archive, was a complex and multi-talented man. A devout Quaker and a highly successful Victorian businessman, he was philosophical by nature and pioneering in outlook. By 1855 he had already established a wholesale grocery business in Liverpool, and sold it for the astonishing sum of £200,000, which is the equivalent today of over £15,000,000. Now in his thirties, and captivated by the new science of photography, Frith set out on a series of pioneering journeys up the Nile and to the Near East.

INTRIGUE AND EXPLORATION

He was the first photographer to venture beyond the sixth cataract of the Nile. Africa was still the mysterious 'Dark Continent', and Stanley and Livingstone's historic meeting was a decade into the future. The conditions for picture taking confound belief. He laboured for hours in his wicker dark-room in the sweltering heat of the desert, while the volatile chemicals fizzed dangerously in their trays. Back in London he exhibited his photographs and was 'rapturously cheered' by members of the Royal Society. His reputation as a photographer was made overnight.

VENTURE OF A LIFE-TIME

By the 1870s the railways had threaded their way across the country, and Bank Holidays and half-day Saturdays had been made obligatory by Act of Parliament. All of a sudden the working man and his family were able to enjoy days out, take holidays, and see a little more of the world.

With typical business acumen, Francis Frith foresaw that these new tourists would enjoy having souvenirs to commemorate their days out. For the next thirty years he travelled the country by train and by pony and trap, producing fine photographs of seaside resorts and beauty spots that were keenly bought by millions of Victorians. These prints were painstakingly pasted into family albums and pored over during the dark nights of winter, rekindling precious memories of summer excursions. Frith's studio was soon supplying retail shops all over the country, and by 1890 F Frith & Co had become the greatest specialist photographic publishing company in the world, with over 2,000 sales outlets, and pioneered the picture postcard.

FRANCIS FRITH'S LEGACY

Francis Frith had died in 1898 at his villa in Cannes, his great project still growing. By 1970 the archive he created contained over a third of a million pictures showing 7,000 British towns and villages.

Frith's legacy to us today is of immense significance and value, for the magnificent archive of evocative photographs he created provides a unique record of change in the cities, towns and villages throughout Britain over a century and more. Frith and his fellow studio photographers revisited locations many times down the years to update their views, compiling for us an enthralling and colourful pageant of British life and character.

We are fortunate that Frith was dedicated to recording the minutiae of everyday life. For it is this sheer wealth of visual data, the painstaking chronicle of changes in dress, transport, street layouts, buildings, housing and landscape that captivates us so much today, offering us a powerful link with the past and with the lives of our ancestors.

Computers have now made it possible for Frith's many thousands of images to be accessed almost instantly. The archive offers every one of us an opportunity to examine the places where we and our families have lived and worked down the years. Its images, depicting our shared past, are now bringing pleasure and enlightenment to millions around the world a century and more after his death.

For further information visit: www.francisfrith.com

INTERIOR DECORATION

Frith's photographs can be seen framed and as giant wall murals in thousands of pubs, restaurants, hotels, banks, retail stores and other public buildings throughout Britain. These provide interesting and attractive décor, generating strong local interest and acting as a powerful reminder of gentler days in our increasingly busy and frenetic world.

FRITH PRODUCTS

All Frith photographs are available as prints and posters in a variety of different sizes and styles. In the UK we also offer a range of other gift and stationery products illustrated with Frith photographs, although many of these are not available for delivery outside the UK – see our web site for more information on the products available for delivery in your country.

THE INTERNET

Over 100,000 photographs of Britain can be viewed and purchased on the Frith web site. The web site also includes memories and reminiscences contributed by our customers, who have personal knowledge of localities and of the people and properties depicted in Frith photographs. If you wish to learn more about a specific town or village you may find these reminiscences fascinating to browse. Why not add your own comments if you think they would be of interest to others? See **www.francisfrith.com**

PLEASE HELP US BRING FRITH'S PHOTOGRAPHS TO LIFE

Our authors do their best to recount the history of the places they write about. They give insights into how particular towns and villages developed, they describe the architecture of streets and buildings, and they discuss the lives of famous people who lived there. But however knowledgeable our authors are, the story they tell is necessarily incomplete.

Frith's photographs are so much more than plain historical documents. They are living proofs of the flow of human life down the generations. They show real people at real moments in history; and each of those people is the son or daughter of someone, the brother or sister, aunt or uncle, grandfather or grandmother of someone else. All of them lived, worked and played in the streets depicted in Frith's photographs.

We would be grateful if you would give us your insights into the places shown in our photographs: the streets and buildings, the shops, businesses and industries. Post your memories of life in those streets on the Frith website: what it was like growing up there, who ran the local shop and what shopping was like years ago; if your workplace is shown tell us about your working day and what the building is used for now. Read other visitors' memories and reconnect with your shared local history and heritage. With your help more and more Frith photographs can be brought to life, and vital memories preserved for posterity, and for the benefit of historians in the future.

Wherever possible, we will try to include some of your comments in future editions of our books. Moreover, if you spot errors in dates, titles or other facts, please let us know, because our archive records are not always completely accurate—they rely on 140 years of human endeavour and hand-compiled records. You can email us using the contact form on the website.

Thank you!

For further information, trade, or author enquiries
please contact us at the address below:

**The Francis Frith Collection, 6 Oakley Business Park,
Wylye Road, Dinton, Wiltshire SP3 5EU.**

Tel: +44 (0)1722 716 376 Fax: +44 (0)1722 716 881
e-mail: sales@francisfrith.co.uk **www.francisfrith.com**